John F. KENNEDY

DAVID DOWNING

H www.heinemann.co.uk/library
Visit our website to find out more information about Heinemann Library books.

To order:
☎ Phone 44 (0) 1865 888066
🖹 Send a fax to 44 (0) 1865 314091
💻 Visit the Heinemann Bookshop at www.heinemann.co.uk/library to browse our
catalogue and order online.

First published in Great Britain by Heinemann Library,
Halley Court, Jordan Hill, Oxford OX2 8EJ,
a division of Reed Educational and Professional Publishing Ltd.
Heinemann is a registered trademark of Reed Educational and Professional Publishing Ltd.

OXFORD MELBOURNE AUCKLAND
JOHANNESBURG BLANTYRE GABORONE
IBADAN PORTSMOUTH (NH) USA CHICAGO

Designed by AMR
Originated by Dot Gradations
Printed in China

ISBN 0 431 13853 2
05 04 03 02 01
10 9 8 7 6 5 4 3 2 1

British Library Cataloguing in Publication Data
Downing, David
John F. Kennedy. – (Leading lives)
1.Kennedy, John F. (John Fitzgerald), 1917–1963 – Juvenile
literature 2.Presidents – United States – Biography –
Juvenile literature 3.United States – Politics and
government – 1945–1989 – Juvenile literature 4.United
States – History – 1945– – Juvenile literature
1.Title
973.9'22'092

Acknowledgements
The publishers would like to thank the following for permission to reproduce photographs: AKG Photo:
pp. 26, 49; Associated Press: pp. 20, 37; Corbis: pp. 6, 13, 14, 16, 22, 25, 29, 33, 39, 44, 45, 52, 55; Hulton
Getty: pp. 10, 11, 30, 31, 36, 42, 50, 51; JFK Archives: p. 47; Popperfoto: pp. 15, 18, 23, 46;
Popperfoto/Reuters: p. 4; The John F. Kennedy Library: p. 9.

Cover photograph reproduced with permission of Archive Photos.

Our thanks to Christopher Gibb for his comments in the preparation of this book.

Every effort has been made to contact copyright holders of any material reproduced in this book.
Any omissions will be rectified in subsequent printings if notice is given to the publishers.

Any words appearing in the text in bold, **like this**, are explained in the Glossary.

Contents

1 Death in the afternoon 4

2 Childhood and youth 6

3 War hero 12

4 Congressman 15

5 President 19

6 Taking on the Soviet Union 24

7 The 'rising peoples' 28

8 Taking care of America 32

9 In the White House 36

10 The Cuban Missile Crisis 40

11 Civil rights 43

12 The last six months 48

13 Kennedy's legacy 52

Timeline 56

Key people of Kennedy's time 58

The US system of government – at a glance 59

Places to visit and further reading 60

Glossary 61

Index 64

1 Death in the afternoon

In the early afternoon of 22 November 1963, John F. Kennedy was riding in an open-top car through the Texan city of Dallas. He was smiling and waving at the large crowds that had gathered to welcome him, when the shots rang out. One caught him in the neck, the other in the head. As the car raced for the nearest hospital, his wife cradled his head in her arms, hoping against hope, but the surgeons could do nothing. Twenty-five minutes after his arrival, the 35th president of the USA was pronounced dead. He was 46 years old.

▲ President Kennedy and his wife Jackie riding through the streets of Dallas moments before the fatal shots were fired. Texas Governor John Connally is sitting directly in front of the President.

As the news of his death spread around America and the world, it produced an outpouring of shock and grief. In a few short years John Kennedy – or Jack, as he was usually known – had come to stand for all that seemed young, daring and alive in a world that was finally emerging from the long shadow of World War II. It was hard to believe that he was dead, harder still to accept that he had been struck down by an assassin's bullet.

Americans of all ages grieved for their young leader, the handsome war hero with the beautiful wife and the two young children, who had given their country a dynamic new image in the world. Black Americans grieved for the president who had, after much hesitation and against his own political interests, finally joined them in the struggle to end racial discrimination.

On the other side of the Atlantic, Europeans grieved for something less specific – a young life cut short, a promise denied. In London a huge crowd gathered outside the American Embassy to salute his memory; in West Berlin lighted candles were placed in thousands of darkened windows. Even in Moscow, capital of the **Cold War** enemy, there was grief. Nikita Khrushchev, the Soviet leader who had gone eyeball to eyeball with Kennedy in the Cuban Missile Crisis, reportedly broke down and wept when he heard the news.

What was so extraordinary about this man? Where had this tidal wave of grief come from? Had he really achieved so much, or had his qualities been magnified by the shock of his death? Or had he simply touched a chord among human hearts which reverberated beyond his own country and time?

Childhood and youth

In October 1914 two prominent Catholic, Irish-American and Bostonian families were united by the marriage of Joseph Kennedy and Rose Fitzgerald. Their first son, born the following year, was named after his father. The second, born 29 May 1917 in the Boston suburb of Brookline, was named John Fitzgerald. Like many of those named John, he would always be known as 'Jack' to his family and friends.

Joe and Rose Kennedy went on to have nine children – five sisters and two more brothers arriving to join Joe Junior and Jack. One sister, Rosemary, had learning difficulties from birth, but all the children were born into a highly prosperous family, and their father continued to make the most of his many business opportunities. By the beginning of the 1930s he had invested a million dollars for each child, for their use in later life.

▶ Brothers and best friends. Joe Junior and John (Jack) Kennedy at the family's summer home in Hyannisport, off the coast of the state of Massachusetts, 1925.

The Kennedy children

Joe and Rose Kennedy had nine children in all. The first, Joseph (known as Joe Junior), was born in 1915. John (known as Jack) came along two years later, in 1917. In 1918 a daughter, Rosemary, was born, followed by three others, Kathleen in 1920, Eunice in 1921 and Patricia in 1924. In 1925 Robert (known as Bobby) was born. In 1928 Jean was born and the ninth and last child, Edward, was born in 1932.

Growing up

The Kennedy children grew up in a world of privilege, of private nurses and governesses. The only non-white faces they saw belonged to servants. When the holidays came around, the family moved from big houses in Boston or New York to one of their equally enormous seaside properties in Massachusetts and Florida.

However, the children did not grow up in a world of idle luxury. Jack's father allowed no small talk at the family dinner table – his children were expected to keep up with the news of the day and, from an early age, to be able to discuss it intelligently. The family's enormous wealth, and the acceptance of inequality which went with it, were both taken for granted, but so too was the belief that Kennedys should be actively involved – preferably as leaders – in the political and economic life of the community. The Kennedy children were expected to prepare themselves for such responsibility in later life. The constant pursuit of perfection created a highly competitive family atmosphere. A Kennedy was not expected to easily accept defeat or failure – life was about winning.

Because of their closeness in age, the two oldest boys competed mostly with each other. It was an uneven contest. Joe Junior was two years older, more academically gifted, better at sports, and very healthy. Jack, on the other hand, always seemed to be sick with one illness or another, although the doctors could not work out why. He rarely allowed this to spoil his natural cheerfulness, but many long absences certainly affected his school and college careers. In his heart of hearts, he must have often hated being such an invalid in a family that placed so much importance on success.

Away at school

Jack went to local schools until he was 13, but was then sent away from home for the first time, to a private boarding school in Connecticut, about $2\frac{1}{4}$ hours' drive from Boston. His first year was interrupted by acute appendicitis, and his parents decided he should start the next year at Choate School, which his brother Joe was already attending. Over the next four years, as most of America scraped along the bottom of the **Great Depression**, an often-sickly Jack struggled to match his brother's achievements in the classrooms and on the sports fields of this exclusive private school.

He failed on both counts, but the teachers recognized his obvious intelligence and he was very popular among his fellow pupils. He and a friend formed a secret club called 'the Muckers' which specialized in imaginative practical jokes, and on one occasion his father was called to see the headmaster to hear warnings of possible expulsion. Jack got down to some serious studying in his fourth and final year, but still only managed to graduate 64th in a class of 112.

College years

Jack was 18 now and, like his brother before him, he was sent across the Atlantic to study at the London School of Economics. Once again he fell ill, this time with a blood infection, and he was forced to cut the school year short and return to America. He decided he would rather enrol at Princeton University, where most of his Choate friends had gone, than join Joe at Harvard. However, his appendicitis flared up again, forcing him to cancel these plans as well. In the summer of 1936 he decided that it was better to start afresh at Harvard, studying **political science**, than to begin again at Princeton a year behind his friends.

His academic work continued to be uninspired, but he threw himself into college life, and was soon organizing entertainments and writing for the student paper. His old dreams of success on the football field were finally ended when he suffered a serious back injury during a game, and new dreams of swimming glory were put to rest by a viral infection. He must have sometimes wondered whether he had used up all his life's luck in being born into such a privileged family.

▲ John Kennedy (standing third from left) tried out for the Harvard swimming team in his junior year after a back injury forced him to give up football.

In 1938 his father was appointed **ambassador** to Great Britain, and Jack was given what amounted to a front-seat view of Europe sliding towards war. The Harvard authorities were willing to let him spend several months learning about international politics at first hand, and his father was pleased to have such a helper. Jack visited many European countries as his father's unofficial researcher, and in 1939 he spent several months working in the London Embassy as a political secretary. He was even present in the British House of Commons on the day war was declared against Germany.

Back home he wrote a thesis (long essay) on how unprepared Britain was to fight a war. His Harvard teachers were impressed enough to graduate him with honours, and the thesis was published as a small book entitled *Why England Slept*.

◀ *John Kennedy and his father Joseph Kennedy, then ambassador in Great Britain, boarding a plane for Paris at London's Croydon Airport in March 1939.*

Joseph Kennedy

Jack Kennedy's father was a bank president before he was 30, a highly successful speculator on the **stock market**, and, according to many, a major player in the bootlegging industry (the illegal transport and sale of alcohol). In the 1930s he followed family tradition (both his father Patrick and Rose's father John 'Honey Fitz' Fitzgerald had been political celebrities in Boston) and became heavily involved in politics. He filled two important government posts under President Roosevelt and in 1937 he was appointed US ambassador to Great Britain.

In this last job he made himself deeply unpopular, both in London and Washington. He thought that joining Britain and France in a war against Germany would be bad for American business, and despite the growing evidence of German crimes against the Jews he refused to admit that there was any moral or practical case for opposing them. President Roosevelt did not share these views, and Joseph was forced to resign as ambassador early in 1941.

When, later that year, the USA was forced into the war by the Japanese attack on the US naval base at Pearl Harbor, it became obvious that for once in his life Joe Kennedy had backed the wrong horse. He now knew that he would never be president, and would have to settle for putting his first-born son into the White House.

▲ *The Kennedy family in London's Green Park, 1939. From left: Eunice, John (known as Jack), Rosemary, Jean, Joseph, Edward, Rose, Joseph Jr, Pat, Robert, Kathleen.*

3 | War hero

War was coming to America. Joe Junior would be accepted by any of the armed services he cared to join, but Jack knew he would have trouble passing the medical tests any of them would require. Early in 1941 he began a five-month programme of exercises aimed at strengthening his back. The thought of missing out on the fighting once it started was more than he could bear.

The exercises paid off, but not quite as well as he had hoped. While Joe Junior flew planes for the Navy, Jack was stuck in a Washington desk job working for Naval Intelligence. During this time he began a love affair with Inga Arvad, a Danish journalist who had friends in the German government. There is no evidence that Inga was a spy, but Kennedy's attachment was far from wise. It would not be the last time he showed himself ready to risk his future for the sake of his love life.

He was transferred to Charleston, South Carolina, where he taught safety procedures to defence workers. The work was useful but boring. Longing for active service, he received permission from the Navy to get his back fixed once and for all. After undergoing several months of treatment at the Chelsea Naval Hospital in Boston, he was declared fit. For the rest of 1942 he trained as a PT (or patrol torpedo) boat commander. When the Navy tried to keep him on as an instructor at the end of his training, Kennedy finally lost patience, and got his father to pull a few strings. By March 1943 he was on his way across the Pacific. On arrival in the Solomon Islands, he was given command of his own boat, the *PT 109*.

▲ Kennedy aboard the PT boat he commanded in the Pacific during 1943.

Action in the Pacific

The next four months were spent patrolling channels between those islands held by the two sides, and trying to intercept the enemy convoys which supplied those held by the Japanese. On 19 July, *PT 109* was spotted and bombed by an enemy plane, and flying shrapnel seriously injured two of Kennedy's men.

Two weeks later, on the night of 1 August, *PT 109* was patrolling at sea when a Japanese destroyer loomed out of the night, sliced the American boat diagonally in two, and continued on its way. Two of Kennedy's men were killed, others badly burned. The living clung to the wreckage for hours, but no rescuers arrived. Kennedy decided that they should make for the nearest island, which was over 5 kilometres (3 miles) away. One man was too badly burned to swim, and Kennedy towed him the whole way.

There was neither food nor water on the island, and their signals for help went unanswered. Kennedy coaxed all the surviving members of his group through another 5 kilometres (3 miles) of water to a larger island, but the green coconuts they found to eat there made them sick. Kennedy and another man swam on to a third island, where they found a dugout canoe, a drum of water and a little food. Returning to the second island, they discovered native visitors. Kennedy scratched a message on a coconut husk – 'Native knows posit[ion]. He can pilot. 11 alive. Need small boat. Kennedy' – and asked them to deliver it. A few hours later *PT 157* arrived to pick up the stranded crew.

Kennedy received a Navy and Marine Corps medal for 'outstanding courage, endurance and leadership in keeping

with the highest traditions of the US Naval Service'. He also discovered that he had badly re-injured his back, and by December it was obvious that his days of active service were over. By the late spring of 1944, he was back in hospital, and it was there, in early August, that he received the news of his older brother's death in Europe. It was now up to him to fulfil his father's dreams.

◀ *Naval Lieutenant John F. Kennedy in 1944.*

4 Congressman

As the war came to an end, Jack Kennedy readied himself for a political career. When a Boston House of Representatives seat became vacant in 1946, he announced that he would be a candidate for the **Democratic Party nomination**.

FOR A SUMMARY OF THE US SYSTEM OF GOVERNMENT, SEE PAGE 59.

Despite his youth and lack of experience, he won it quite easily, and went on to claim the **safe seat** in the actual election. His war record and his family's long association with the city had helped him, but the key ingredient in his success had been his father's money. Joe Kennedy had spared no expense in getting Jack over this first difficult hurdle of his political career.

In 1947 Jack was finally diagnosed as suffering from Addison's Disease, which weakens the body's immune system. Here, it seemed, was the reason for all those lasting illnesses of his childhood and youth. The diagnosis itself was good news: the disease, though incurable, was controllable with the right medication. Its impact on Kennedy's life could now be lessened.

► *Kennedy is sworn in as a US senator after his election victory in November 1952.*

15

Kennedy served for six years in the House of Representatives. His record was far from spectacular, but he showed himself more of a **liberal** on most issues than his father had been. He campaigned against slum housing and opposed a bill that put further limits on workers' rights to strike. In 1952 he decided to stand for the more prestigious Senate, and once again his father's money and organizational skills made the difference. He defeated the popular Henry Cabot Lodge by over 70,000 votes.

During the campaign he met Jacqueline ('Jackie') Bouvier, the 23-year-old daughter of a wealthy Wall Street financier, and in September of the following year they were married. The wedding received widespread press coverage and 3000 intruders had to be turned away by police.

▲ *John and Jackie Kennedy outside St Mary's Church, Newport, Rhode Island, after their wedding on 12 September 1953.*

Senator Kennedy

Kennedy was now becoming a national celebrity, his future looking brighter with each passing year. His back condition, though, had not improved. During 1954 it grew so bad that he was forced to use crutches, and over the following winter he underwent several life-threatening operations in an attempt to put matters right. Twice he was ill enough to receive the last rites (special prayers for the dying offered by a priest of the Catholic religion), but each time he pulled through. The operations produced only a slight improvement, and Kennedy's back remained a problem for the rest of his life.

During these long months he found time to research and write a book about eight US senators, all of whom had bravely supported unpopular policies. *Profiles of Courage* won a **Pulitzer Prize** in 1957, and its message, that conscience should come before self-interest, was one that Kennedy would always seek to promote.

In 1956 he narrowly missed selection as Adlai Stevenson's **running mate** in the presidential campaign. This proved a blessing in disguise, as he escaped being tarnished by the **incumbent** President Eisenhower's defeat of Stevenson. In 1958 he completed his first term as a senator and was re-elected with an overwhelming majority. Few now doubted that he would run for the presidency in 1960.

There had been sadness at home when his and Jackie's first child was stillborn, but just over a year later Jackie gave birth to a healthy daughter, whom they named Caroline. Three years later, their son John would be born, completing the picture of America's perfect family – young, good-looking and successful.

▲ Kennedy and his wife Jackie campaigning for the presidency on the streets of New York City, October 1960.

Seeking the nomination

There were several obstacles in Kennedy's path to the presidency. He was very young – only 43 in 1960 – and he had only a moderate record as a member of **Congress**. There was always the possibility of a sex scandal if any of his many secret affairs was to be revealed. Above all, there was his religion. A Catholic had never been elected president, and the Democratic Party was reluctant to risk nominating one.

Kennedy and his father decided that everything depended on success in the **primaries**. They spent a lot of money on advertising and made good use of new **opinion polling** techniques. Kennedy confronted the Catholic issue head on, insisting that his religion would not affect the way he conducted himself as president. By the time the Party **convention** opened, he had enough votes to be sure of the nomination.

The new frontier

'We stand today on the edge of a new frontier – the frontier of the 1960s, a frontier of unknown opportunities and paths, a frontier of unfulfilled hopes and threats.... The new frontier of which I speak is not a set of promises – it is a set of challenges. It sums up not what I intend to offer the American people, but what I intend to ask of them.'

(From Kennedy's nomination acceptance speech, 1960)

5 President

Kennedy's campaign for the presidency in the summer and autumn of 1960 followed the pattern of his campaign for the **nomination**. His team, led by his brother Bobby and guided by his father Joe, planned everything down to the last possible detail. Advertising campaigns stressed his young and dynamic image, **opinion polls** and the new computers were used to analyse voting trends. The candidate criss-crossed the country speaking at meeting after meeting.

Kennedy's platform

What was he saying? His social policies sounded more **liberal** than those of his opponent Richard Nixon but there was not much detail – he could not afford to antagonize **Democratic Party** supporters in **the South** by sounding too liberal. He was particularly careful when it came to talking about **civil rights** for America's ethnic minorities, although he did make a point of helping African-American leader Martin Luther King Junior when he was briefly jailed for organizing demonstrations in Georgia.

FOR DETAILS ON KEY PEOPLE OF KENNEDY'S TIME, SEE PAGE 58.

Kennedy was also cautious when it came to economic matters, and in foreign affairs he adopted an even more aggressively patriotic position than Nixon. These were years in which many Americans worried that they were falling behind the Soviet Union, particularly when it came to military strength and space exploration. They had also been alarmed by the recent revolution in Cuba, and its apparent drift towards **Communism**. Kennedy played very strongly on these cards during the campaign. The **Republican Party** had done nothing about these dangers, he said. He, on the other hand, would deal with Cuba, and he would close the **'missile gap'** between the USA and the Soviet Union.

▲ *The live TV broadcast of the debate between Richard Nixon and John F. Kennedy on 21 October 1960.*

His youthful energy and enthusiasm may have been more important than any particular policy. Many Americans were ready for change, and Kennedy seemed more willing to deliver it than Nixon. Watching the candidates' debate on TV, a majority of the American public also found him more honest, more charming and more likeable.

Victory

The election still proved close. Kennedy received only a small majority of the votes that were cast, and doubts were raised about the honesty of even this narrow margin. In the crucial state of Illinois there were loud and probably justified complaints that the vote had been rigged in his favour. They were ignored. He had won, and Joe Kennedy's dream of a son in the White House had come true. Three weeks later, Jack had a son of his own. Jackie gave birth to John Junior on 25 November.

There would be one family member in Kennedy's **Cabinet** – brother Bobby, though only 35, was Jack's choice for **Attorney General**. Two Republicans – Robert McNamara and McGeorge Bundy – were given the important posts of Defence Secretary and Foreign Affairs Adviser. Most of Kennedy's choices were young, and all were white males. His only attempt to appoint an African-American was prevented by **Congress**, and no women were ever included in his Cabinet. There were clearly limits to how much change he wanted, but for the moment everyone seemed too caught up in the excitement to care.

Robert Kennedy

Robert (Bobby) was the third son of Joe and Rose Kennedy. After serving in World War II, he trained as a lawyer, and in the late 1950s he worked as a prosecutor for the Senate Select Committee on Improper Activities, which investigated connections between **organized crime** and the labour unions. He managed his brother's campaign in 1960, and as Attorney General (1961–64) he made sure that civil rights campaigners had the backing of the law. Throughout Jack Kennedy's presidency, Bobby acted as his brother's confidant and right-hand man, someone with whom he could always share his thoughts.

Early days

Kennedy's **inaugural speech**, delivered on a snow-strewn morning in January 1961, was a triumph. Jointly scripted by Kennedy and his adviser Ted Sorensen, it scaled heights of **rhetoric** that were truly inspiring. On close examination, much of it seemed overblown, not to mention essentially untrue – how, for example, did the descendants of slaves feel when they heard Kennedy claim that the USA had always been committed to human rights? However, few Americans picked the speech apart. Most simply shared in the pride and the promise of better to come.

The new Peace Corps, which Kennedy had begun to promote in the last week of the campaign, reflected the message of the inaugural speech. This organization for sending young Americans out into the poorer parts of the world, where they would spend two years doing whatever jobs their hosts most required, went into operation in the summer of 1961. It was a typical Kennedy idea. The world's poor would be helped, and young Americans would widen their knowledge. There would be an improvement in America's image, which would help in the worldwide fight against Communism.

This was only one of many exciting initiatives implemented during Kennedy's first few months in office. The way he encouraged press criticism, his introduction of televised press conferences, and his immediate measures to ease the poverty in West Virginia, which had so shocked him on the campaign trail, all gave substance to the notion that here was a new and vigorous broom, one that would sweep aside the cobwebs of the Eisenhower era that had preceded it.

▼ *After signing the bill creating the Peace Corps, President Kennedy hands the pen to the organization's first director, Sargent Shriver.*

'Ask not what your country can do for you...'

'Let the word go forth from this time and place, to friend and foe alike, that the torch has passed to a new generation of Americans... proud of our ancient heritage, and unwilling to witness or permit the slow undoing of those human rights to which this nation has always been committed and to which we are committed today at home and around the world.

Let every nation know, whether it wishes us well or ill, that we shall pay any price, bear any burden, meet any hardship, support any friend, oppose any foe to assure the survival and success of liberty.

'In the long history of the world only a few generations have been granted the role of defending freedom in its hour of maximum danger... The energy, the faith and the devotion, which we bring to this endeavour, will light our country and all who serve in it and the glow from that fire can truly light the world.

'And so, my fellow Americans, ask not what your country will do for you. Ask what you can do for your country.'

(From Kennedy's inaugural speech, 20 January 1961)

▶ *Two of the first Peace Corps workers in East Pakistan (now Bangladesh) preparing to board a train in the city of Dhaka in November 1961.*

Kennedy had no thoughts of ending the **Cold War** – he wanted to win it. He realized that in the nuclear age a military victory was impossible, but he thought that there were other ways of coming out on top. If the USA defended itself effectively, he said, eventually the 'disease of liberty' would infect the **Communist** world. His great fear, as he repeatedly told the American people during the 1960 election campaign, was that the country was not defending itself adequately, and that not enough effort was being taken to spread the 'disease of liberty'.

The Cold War before Kennedy

The Cold War was the name given to the uneasy peace that existed between the **free enterprise** world (led by the USA) and the Communist world (led by the Soviet Union) between World War II and the collapse of the Soviet Union in 1991. Mutual distrust hardened into outright hostility during the European disputes of 1947–49, and this hostility was further deepened through the 1950s by continuous **propaganda**, a nuclear arms race, and a series of **proxy conflicts** between the allies of the two superpowers in the developing world, of which the Korean War (1950–53) was the most important.

Accelerating the arms race

During the campaign Kennedy had claimed that there was a 'missile gap' – the USA was falling behind the Soviet Union in missile production and deployment. When he came to office, he discovered that there was no such gap, that the Soviet missile force was actually much, much smaller than he had been told. However, he and Defence Secretary Robert McNamara convinced themselves that it was important to preserve this huge advantage, and just to make absolutely sure, they decided to go ahead with a huge new programme of missile construction.

Some consider this one of the most irresponsible actions Kennedy ever took. Not surprisingly, the Soviets decided that they would have to start a huge programme of their own, and the greatest **arms race** in history was set in motion, threatening human survival and consuming money that both governments could have used to better effect elsewhere.

Building the Wall

The one place where the USA and the Soviet Union confronted each other directly was Berlin. In early 1961, worried by the growing number of East Germans moving to the West, the Soviet leadership began proposing measures which would isolate West Berlin from the rest of West Germany.

The Soviet leader Nikita Khrushchev (see page 58) repeated these threats at his Vienna Summit meeting with Kennedy in April 1961. Kennedy had hoped that a personal relationship with the Soviet leader would make the possibility of dangerous misunderstandings less likely, but he had never experienced anything like Khrushchev's bullying tactics. Though shaken by the encounter, he held his and America's ground. When, later in the year, the Russians came up with another solution to their problem – a high wall to keep the East Germans in – Kennedy wisely did nothing. He realized that this was a defensive move, and he knew that the wall would be terrible publicity for his Communist enemy.

▲ Kennedy meets Soviet Premier Khrushchev (on the left) at the US Embassy in Vienna, June 1961.

Berlin

After World War II, the German capital Berlin was divided into Russian, American, British and French zones of occupation. With the onset of the Cold War, the three Western zones became West Berlin, the Soviet zone East Berlin. Since the whole city was situated inside Soviet-controlled East Germany, West Berlin became a Western island in a Communist sea. In 1948–49 the Soviets tried to force the Western powers out of the 'island' by means of a **blockade**, but the attempt was defeated by an airlift.

Through the 1950s West Berlin became an increasingly prosperous advertisement for free enterprise in the heart of East Germany, and the obvious first stop for those who wished to escape from Communism. In 1961 more and more East Germans started crossing the border into West Berlin. Since these tended to be the most qualified people, their departures created a grave threat to both the East German economy and the entire Soviet bloc.

▲ *East German troops engaged in building the Berlin Wall. This construction work, undertaken in response to the growing flood of people leaving for the West, began on 13 August 1961.*

Struggle for superiority

Both Kennedy and Khrushchev understood that the Cold War would not be won or lost in Europe. The two systems would be judged on their economic performance and their progress in science and technology. Space was one obvious area of competition. The Soviet triumphs of the late 1950s had alarmed Americans, and Kennedy was determined to catch and surpass them. In May 1961, a month after Yuri Gagarin became the first man in space, Kennedy pledged that the USA would 'land a man on the moon and return him safely to earth before the decade is out'.

All these contests were important, but according to Kennedy the decisive battles of the Cold War would be fought out in those parts of the world that currently held no allegiance to either side. This battle for the **developing world** would occupy much of his time as president.

7 The 'rising peoples'

'The great battleground for the defence and expansion of freedom today', Kennedy said early in 1961, 'is the whole southern half of the globe… the lands of the rising peoples.' How did he intend to win that battle?

Sticks and carrots

Firstly, Kennedy was keen to transform the US armed forces. Nuclear weapons were necessary to deter the Soviet Union from invading other countries, but they were no use against **guerrilla fighters** or urban **terrorists**. America needed what he called a 'flexible response' capability. In particular, it needed **counter-insurgency troops** with the military skills to defeat the enemy and the medical and teaching skills to win over the local population. This was the only way to win the **guerrilla wars** that were being fought in the countryside in the **developing world**.

For all his idealism, Kennedy was a ruthless man. It was alleged that Guyanese leader Cheddi Jagan was driven from power by a **CIA**-financed campaign after he told Kennedy that he believed in **state planning**. The Dominican Republic's President Trujillo and Congolese politician Patrice Lumumba were both killed by American agencies during Kennedy's presidency, and there is no doubt that strenuous attempts were made to assassinate Cuba's Fidel Castro (see page 58). Some have claimed that Kennedy himself had no direct knowledge of these events, but there is evidence which suggests otherwise.

These were the sticks Kennedy used to get what he wanted, but he used carrots as well. The Peace Corps won friends for the USA by helping people, and it offered proof of America's increasing interest in the developing world. On an even grander scale, in 1961 Kennedy launched the Alliance for Progress, an enormous package of economic aid for Latin America. A prosperous continent, he thought, would have no interest in **Communism**.

Laos and Cuba

All these policies would take time to work, and Kennedy faced a succession of crises from the moment he took office. The first concerned a **proxy conflict** in Laos, a small South-east Asian country next to Vietnam. The Russians were sending arms to the Communists there, and the Americans were doing the same for the government forces. Kennedy could either up the stakes and send American troops, abandon the country to the Communists, or work out a compromise solution with the Soviets. He wisely chose the latter. Laos itself had no real importance to either superpower.

▲ At a press conference in March 1961 Kennedy points out the extent of Communist infiltration in the South-east Asian country of Laos.

Another problem Kennedy inherited from the Eisenhower administration was America's deteriorating relationship with Castro's Cuba. During the presidential campaign, Kennedy had frequently demanded action against Cuba, and once in office he agreed that an invasion planned under his predecessor should go ahead. In April 1961 a force of Cuban **exiles**, supported by US planes, landed at the Bay of Pigs. It was a disaster. There was no popular support for the invaders, all of whom were killed or taken prisoner. Kennedy looked very foolish, and for the rest of his life he would seek revenge against Castro, sponsoring assassination attempts and a campaign of disruption and sabotage called Operation Mongoose.

Cuba

In 1958–59 Fidel Castro led a successful and overwhelmingly popular revolution on this Caribbean island. It was not, in its early years, a Communist revolution, but the Cuban economy was largely run and owned by Americans, and if Castro's government wished to improve the prospects of ordinary Cubans, it had no choice but to take decisions that angered the American business community. The USA accused Castro of Communism, and eventually retaliated by refusing to let Cuba sell its sugar – which accounted for over 90% of Cuba's national earnings – in the USA .

The Soviet Union then offered to buy the sugar instead. The Cubans accepted, which made the Americans even more convinced that they were Communists. By late 1960 a decision had been taken in Washington to support an armed invasion of the island by Cuban exiles.

◀ *Cuban leader Fidel Castro, who came to power as the result of a popular revolution in January 1959.*

A failure to understand

Kennedy's policies towards the developing world were based on a failure to understand how things in those countries worked. He wanted to see the 'rising peoples' rise, but he could not understand that what was good business for his own country was often bad news for others. There were real conflicts of interest, as the fate of the Alliance for Progress made clear. This $20 billion package of aid sounded very generous, but most of the money was in the form of loans, and all of it had to be spent on goods from the USA. Not surprisingly, most Latin Americans derived little benefit from the scheme.

The worst consequence of his lack of understanding was the way he deepened the US commitment to South Vietnam. The government there was very unpopular, but, as far as Kennedy and his advisers could see, the only alternative was a Communist takeover. They were determined that should not happen. So more and more Americans were sent to Vietnam, including military advisers to help the South Vietnamese Army in the jungle and political advisers to prod the government into reforms that would win over the peasantry. The government could not introduce such reforms without putting its own interests and privileges at risk, but Kennedy carried on hoping that it would.

▶ Members of the Special Forces of the US Army, also known as the Green Berets. Kennedy regarded their participation in the Vietnam war as their special mission.

8 Taking care of America

The America that Kennedy had inherited, though rich and prosperous, contained many pockets of great poverty. Around seven per cent of adult Americans were without jobs, and there was widespread **racial discrimination**. The quality of both education and health care provision was very uneven, and in many areas there were no adequate services for the poor. Kennedy, and the **liberals** who made up two-thirds of his **Democratic Party**, were determined to improve matters in all these areas.

FOR A SUMMARY OF THE US SYSTEM OF GOVERNMENT, SEE PAGE 59.

At first sight, the political situation looked promising – the Democrats had a majority in both Houses of **Congress**. The reality was somewhat different. Democrats in **the South** were mostly conservative when it came to social (and particularly racial) matters, and Kennedy could rarely count on their votes. If they and all the **Republican Party** members voted against him, he would not have the majorities he needed.

Economics

At home, Kennedy's first priority was to get the economy right. The rate of growth was slowing and the country's **balance of payments** deficit was likely to be worsened by increased foreign spending on the **Cold War**. Kennedy tried to make America more competitive, to keep its products cheap, by holding down wages and prices. He was equally firm with both sides of industry, successfully defeating wage rises for postal and railroad workers and overturning price rises introduced by the steel bosses.

He also wanted to stimulate the domestic economy with a huge tax cut. He planned to pay for this by increased government borrowing, not by cutting back government spending. This switch to **deficit financing**, which was eventually introduced by his successor Lyndon Johnson, was Kennedy's most important economic contribution.

FOR DETAILS ON KEY PEOPLE OF KENNEDY'S TIME, SEE PAGE 58.

Education

A third of the major proposals Kennedy introduced concerned education. American state schools and colleges were not keeping up with the increased numbers of children and students who attended them. More teachers were needed, more books, and more facilities of all kinds. More assistance was also needed for the increasing numbers who wanted to enter higher education. These young men and women were America's future.

Kennedy's first Education Bill, introduced in 1961, offered the kind of investment which he considered necessary, but it was defeated in Congress by an alliance of Catholic groups (private Catholic schools would not be entitled to any of the money) and Southerners (who feared that any central government intervention in education would lead to **desegregation** in schools). Despite the President's best efforts, similar bills were killed in 1962 and 1963.

▼ *Kennedy addresses a student rally in Milwaukee, Wisconsin during the presidential primary campaign in April 1960.*

33

Health care

Kennedy had a particular interest in health care matters. His sister Rosemary, born with learning difficulties, had spent her adult life in an institution, and the family had long been active in helping similarly afflicted individuals. As president, Jack Kennedy made the issue one of his priorities, and introduced bills that transformed the way people with special needs were treated.

In 1961 his father suffered a disabling stroke. For the last eight years of his life Joseph Kennedy needed the sort of constant care that only the rich could afford, a fact of which his son was well aware. The experience made him more determined to introduce the Democrats' long-favoured **Medicare** scheme of health insurance for senior citizens. His 1962 proposal, bitterly opposed by the American Medical Association, was defeated, but his enthusiastic promotion of the idea would bear fruit after his death.

Achievements and disappointments

The issue of poverty was one that deeply concerned Kennedy. During his first month in office he introduced a series of measures designed to help – a rise in the **minimum wage**, funding for housing projects, benefits for deprived children, and an extension of **unemployment benefits**. Throughout his term he continued to address the problem, but here, and in the closely related field of **civil rights**, he met with intense opposition from Congress. To many Southern Democrats and Republicans, his ideas smacked of **socialism**.

He had many domestic successes. In addition to those already mentioned, he saw that coastlines were protected and water pollution regulated. He got through some of his city improvement and housing plans and he persuaded Congress of the need for new checks on food and drugs.

But the achievements did not match up to the hopes. America, as reflected by Congress, was simply not ready to accept the level of government help for the disadvantaged that Kennedy wanted. He himself had only three years to convince his fellow citizens that he was right, and he always had to bear in mind that re-election in 1964 depended on his not upsetting the electorate too much. Given the size of the obstacles placed in his path, he achieved a great deal in his own right, and his insistence on arguing the case for his proposals over and over again played a big part in their later acceptance.

The problem

'With all of that going for us... with all the pressure and appeals a new President could make, we won by five votes. That shows what we're up against.'

(Kennedy in June 1961, after narrowly winning a crucial vote in Congress)

9 In the White House

Until the arrival of the Kennedys, the 20th-century White House had been a rather stuffy place. It had usually been occupied by couples well into middle age, who had shown little interest in the arts or intellectual pursuits, and whose children had long left home. The Kennedys changed all that. They were both intensely interested in the world beyond politics, and the White House soon became a meeting place for all sorts of entertainers, thinkers and **Nobel Prize** winners. Some even compared Kennedy's Washington to England's mythical Camelot, where the best and brightest had gathered around King Arthur.

Jackie Kennedy played a big part in all this. She was the first young and attractive First Lady anyone could remember; she was sophisticated and intelligent. No one had done anything about the White House itself for years, but she quickly decided to make it 'a museum for our country's traditions, fitted with the very best pictures and furniture'. She discovered a treasure trove of items in the basement and bought other suitable pieces on her travels. While this transformation was underway she hosted a TV tour of the building.

◄ Jackie Kennedy, the First Lady. This picture, taken in 1961, was her first official White House photograph.

The father

She and Jack were proud and involved parents. The burdens of office restricted the time Kennedy could spend with their children, but he obviously enjoyed being a father. Indeed, in this respect he set a fine example to his fellow-American males, who in those days were inclined to leave the business of child-rearing to the children's mothers.

John Junior had been born only two months before they moved into the White House, but was soon to be found hiding and playing under the desk in the presidential office, which is known as the Oval Office. Caroline was often to be seen wandering round the building. On one occasion she told journalists that her Daddy was 'sitting upstairs with his socks and shoes off not doing anything'.

Jack Kennedy's feelings for children, both his own and those of others, are well documented. In 1963 Jackie gave premature birth to a second son, Patrick, who only lived for a few days. Jack, visiting the baby in a Boston hospital, caught sight of two heavily bandaged young girls playing in one of the rooms. When a doctor told him that the girls had been badly burnt, and that one of them might well lose her hand, Kennedy insisted on stopping and writing a note to them.

Secret life

The Kennedys presented the image of a near-perfect family, and at the time that was how Americans saw them. But since Jack Kennedy's death a more complicated picture has come to light. Both before and during his time in the White House he combined an apparently happy family life with almost continuous affairs with other women. Some of them, like the film actress Marilyn Monroe, were as famous as he was. The press knew this was going on, but in those days there was not the same eagerness to hold public figures accountable for their private lives. The American people remained in ignorance of this piece of the Kennedy jigsaw until long after his death.

Day by day

The President's general health was probably better than it had been at any time of his life, but his back continued to give him problems. He usually wore a stiff brace and he had a specially made rocking chair to sit in. His normal working day in the White House began with breakfast and five newspapers at 7.30 a.m., and continued through twelve hours of briefings and conferences, often punctuated by a midday swim.

▶ *John and Robert in conference outside the White House, 1 October 1962.*

On his desk in the Oval Office sat the coconut husk that he had used to send for help in the South Pacific. He often spoke to his father on a specially installed telephone link, and his most frequent companion was brother Bobby, the man whose judgement he trusted most.

Work, family and other relationships took up most of his time, but despite this and the handicap of his problematic back, Kennedy still managed to fit in some of the outdoor pursuits he had always loved so much – sailing, golfing, even riding. No doubt they helped him to forget the worries of office for a while, but for a president of the USA there was no lasting relaxation outside sleep. Wherever Jack Kennedy went, the man who carried the portable telephone and codebook necessary for ordering a nuclear attack followed him.

Showing his age

'On television he looks younger than his age, but 40 million screens are wrong. The figure tapers like a boxer's; the glossy hair is chestnut, with only a suggestion of grey at the temples. The face, however, is deeply lined, especially around the mouth, and the eyes give an even stronger impression of maturity.'

(The journalist William Manchester, after meeting Kennedy early in 1961)

During the year that followed the failed invasion of Cuba in April 1961, Kennedy persisted in his attempts to bring down Castro and his government. Spying was stepped up, aid was sent to **guerrilla fighters** in the Cuban mountains, mines were sabotaged, sugar crops were contaminated. A full **economic embargo** of the island remained in force, and in the summer of 1962 large US naval exercises were held within sight of the Cuban coast.

Kennedy had no intention of allowing another invasion of Cuba, but Castro and his new Soviet friends could hardly be blamed for fearing that one was imminent. Khrushchev realized that he could kill two birds with one stone by putting Soviet missile bases in Cuba – these would both defend the island and shift the **strategic balance** in the Soviet Union's favour. By the late summer of 1962, the construction of these bases was secretly under way.

▲ An aerial view of the construction of a Soviet missile base in Cuba in October 1962.

The discovery

Kennedy was finally shown aerial photographs of the bases on the morning of 16 October. His first decision was to create a committee to oversee the crisis; it was called Ex-Comm and contained around 20 of his **Cabinet** colleagues. For most of the next twelve days, these men argued over the different options open to the President.

It was quickly decided that the USA could not afford to allow the missiles to remain in Cuba. This was an aggressive decision – Cuba had as much right to defend itself as the USA, and the Soviets could point to the fact that the Americans had missiles in Turkey, which were just as close to their own borders. Kennedy and his advisers knew that the military balance had not really been changed, but they were not prepared to accept the loss of face that they thought would follow from simply ignoring these new bases.

They were in fact prepared to risk a nuclear war to get rid of them. 'Your action desperate… no conceivable justification,' the English philosopher Bertrand Russell later wrote to Kennedy.

The gamble

Ex-Comm's decision was to put a naval **blockade** around Cuba, and to seize any missiles that Soviet ships tried to deliver. Kennedy went on TV to tell the nation on the evening of 22 October, and for the next two days, as Soviet ships steamed towards the waiting American blockade, much of the world held its breath. Would the Soviets turn back? Or would a shooting war at sea escalate into a full-scale nuclear exchange?

▲ *The Soviet freighter* Kasimov *photographed by American reconnaissance craft off the coast of Cuba.*

The deal

On 24 October Khrushchev ordered the ships to reverse course, ending the first phase of the crisis. However, the missiles already in Cuba still had to be dealt with before they became operational. Kennedy wanted them out, and his Chiefs of Staff were saying that an invasion could not be long delayed. Fortunately for all concerned, a deal was reached that weekend which left both sides satisfied. Khrushchev agreed to remove the missiles, which gave the Americans what they wanted. Kennedy promised not to invade Cuba, which allowed Khrushchev to claim that he had safeguarded his Cuban ally. In a secret part of the deal, the USA also promised to remove its missiles from Turkey.

Kennedy came out of the crisis with a reputation for toughness, but he was fortunate to do so. It had been his policy towards Cuba that had triggered the whole crisis, and many people both in and outside America were angered by what they saw as his reckless risking of a nuclear war to get his own way.

Moments of terror

'His hand went up and covered his mouth. He opened and closed his fist. His face seemed drawn, his eyes pained, almost grey. We stared at each other across the table.'

(Robert Kennedy describing his brother during the tense days of the Cuban Missile Crisis)

11 Civil rights

Despite his privileged upbringing, Jack Kennedy had an instinctive dislike of the **racial discrimination** which, almost a century after the abolition of slavery, still disfigured his country. He thought it cruel and ridiculous, and hated the way it made America look to the outside world. But he did not want to stake everything on this one issue and completely antagonize the **conservatives**. He needed their support on other important matters, such as education and health.

For the first few months of his presidency he merely picked at the edges of the problem. At his **inauguration** he noticed that there were no black faces among the parading Coast Guards, and immediately took steps to increase African-American enrolment in that organization. He did the same for US embassy staffs around the world. He began trying to convince **Congress** that racial discrimination should be banned in government housing schemes. But he made no move to introduce the sort of far-reaching laws that the **civil rights** leaders were calling for. At this point he was not prepared to go beyond his brother Bobby's promise of 6 May that the Administration would not stand idly by when **racists** ignored or broke existing laws.

The Freedom Riders

This promise was soon tested. Later that month, two mixed-race groups of **Freedom Riders** took two interstate buses through those states in **the South** where **segregation** was still enforced. Their intention was to bring the issue to the nation's attention, and they succeeded. Local racists attacked both buses, leaving one burnt out. The Freedom Riders were badly beaten, both on the road and at the bus terminal in Birmingham, Alabama. Neither the local police nor the forewarned **FBI** came to their aid.

▲ *Guarded by state troopers and National Guardsmen, Freedom Riders board a bus in Montgomery, Alabama en route for Mississippi, 24 May 1961.*

Kennedy's first instinct was to tell the Freedom Riders to give up – he was afraid that their activities would give Khrushchev a **propaganda** victory in the upcoming Vienna Summit. The Freedom Riders took no notice, and Bobby Kennedy sent an assistant to Birmingham to demand their protection. On the next stage of the journey there was more violence, and the assistant was knocked unconscious. An angry Bobby dispatched 500 US marshals to the area, and over the next few months he brought intense pressure to bear on the Interstate Commerce Commission. By the end of the year, America's bus, rail and air terminals had been **desegregated**.

The struggle for civil rights

After the abolition of slavery in 1865, two amendments to the US Constitution (the 14th in 1868, the 15th in 1870) established full citizenship rights for all African-Americans, including the right to vote. However, in some parts of the USA – particularly the South – state governments denied people these rights. The long struggle to make them applicable throughout the country intensified in the 1950s, and culminated in the direct action protests of groups like the Freedom Riders during the Kennedy years.

James Meredith

The issue of civil rights disappeared from the front-page headlines for the better part of a year, but it returned with a vengeance in the summer of 1962. Serious trouble accompanied **voter registration drives** and desegregation campaigns in several southern states, and in September the admission of a young African-American, James Meredith, to the previously segregated University of Mississippi produced another crisis. Jack Kennedy's rather optimistic appeals to the local white population and police were ignored, and once more his brother was forced to send in Federal troops to stop the violence.

This may have been the moment when Kennedy realized that far-reaching action was desperately needed, but he was still reluctant to introduce the necessary bill. He knew it would lose him most of his support in the South, and seriously damage his chances of re-election in 1964. So when he did finally introduce a bill in February 1963, it contained far less than the civil rights leaders wanted. They decided to keep up the pressure with a spring desegregation campaign in Birmingham and a giant march on Washington that summer.

▶ *The Lieutenant Governor of Mississippi, Paul Johnson (wearing glasses), tries to prevent James Meredith (on far right) from entering the University of Mississippi campus, 27 September 1962.*

The moment of truth

The Birmingham campaign was a huge success. All over America people watched as peaceful protesters were set upon by baton-flailing cops and their vicious dogs. Kennedy, who said the sight made him 'sick', now knew he had to act, regardless of the political consequences to himself. On 1 June he told his close advisers that he intended to bring forward a major civil rights bill, banning all racial segregation in public facilities and educational institutions across the country.

On 11 June he appeared on TV to tell the nation. It was one of his finest speeches – eloquent, reasonable and passionately idealistic. 'We owe ourselves a better country,' he told his viewers. It was time to take the great step forward. He knew that he was making his own re-election much more unlikely, but there was no hesitation, no reluctance, in his voice.

The planned march on Washington, which he had earlier described as 'provocative', was allowed to go ahead. After Martin Luther King had delivered his famous 'I have a dream' speech at the Lincoln Monument, he and other civil rights leaders were welcomed at the White House. 'We're in this up to the neck,' Kennedy told them.

◄ *The Reverend Martin Luther King, who was generally acknowledged to be the leader of the African-American civil rights movement until his death by assassination in April 1968.*

Although Kennedy would not live to see the Civil Rights Bill finally pass through Congress in the summer of 1964, it would remain his finest monument.

▼ *Kennedy announcing the Civil Rights Bill on TV on 11 June 1963.*

Announcing the Civil Rights Bill

'We preach freedom around the world, and we mean it, and we cherish our freedom here at home; but are we to say to the world, and much more importantly, to each other, that this is the land of the free except for the Negroes; that we have no second class citizens except Negroes; that we have no class or caste system, no ghettos, no master race except with respect to Negroes... Next week I shall ask the Congress of the United States to act, to make a commitment it has not fully made in this country to the proposition that race has no place in American law or life.'

(From Kennedy's TV address to the nation, 11 June 1963)

12 The last six months

The last six months of Kennedy's presidency saw the adoption of a softer line towards the Soviet Union. The Cuban Missile Crisis in late 1962 had given everyone a shock, and in the following summer a direct telephone link, or 'Hot Line', was installed between the offices of the two leaders. If Kennedy and Khrushchev could just pick up the phone and talk to each other, they believed, there would be less chance of a fatal misunderstanding.

A shift of emphasis

Kennedy was still intent on winning the **Cold War**, but he seemed more aware that any other kind of war between the superpowers would be catastrophic for both. 'In the final analysis', he said in a speech of 25 July 1963, 'we all inhabit this small planet. We all breathe the same air. We all cherish our children's future. And we are all mortal.' His desire for an agreement to end the atmospheric testing of nuclear weapons might have been partly selfish (such a treaty would freeze the huge American lead) but it also reflected his greater awareness of the risk such weapons posed. Khrushchev, keen to concentrate on improving the Soviet economy, was prepared to go along with him. A Test Ban Treaty was signed in July.

When it came to fighting a war of ideas, Kennedy pulled no punches. The Berlin Wall provided the perfect backdrop for a famous speech in the summer of 1963. 'There are many people in the world who really don't understand – or say they don't – the great issue between the free world and the Communist world,' he told a cheering West German crowd. 'Let them come to Berlin!'

▲ *President Kennedy makes his famous 'Let them come to Berlin' speech from the balcony of the Schoeneberg city hall on 26 June 1963.*

Vietnam and the developing world

In the **developing world** Kennedy was much less successful. His government had promised not to invade Cuba, but the secret campaign of harassment continued and the **economic embargo** stayed in place, poisoning relations between the two countries. The Alliance for Progress, which had been intended as a showcase for **free enterprise** and US co-operation with the developing world, was already faltering. 'The problems are almost insuperable,' Kennedy admitted late in 1962. He had no idea how to overcome them.

His most urgent problem was South Vietnam. In the spring of 1963 **Buddhist** groups had begun a series of protests against the Ngo Dinh Diem government (see page 58), and these continued through the summer. Diem, who was also fighting a **guerrilla war** against the **Communists**, clearly had little support in the country, but it seems likely that he was hoping to rescue his fortunes and appease his enemies by declaring South Vietnam neutral and asking the Americans to leave.

At this point a dignified withdrawal seemed a real option for Kennedy, particularly since his only alternative was to support a coup by the South Vietnamese military and continue with a probably unwinnable war. Nevertheless, he chose the second option, not because he thought it made more sense – he was fairly certain it made less – but because he did not believe he could win the 1964 election if he abandoned South Vietnam. Kennedy told close advisers they could get out in 1965, but not before. So Diem was overthrown and killed, the American commitment was increased, and the Vietnamese people were doomed to another twelve years of war.

Death in Dallas

The election of 1964 was much on Kennedy's mind when he travelled to Dallas, Texas in November 1963. In most of the country his popularity was higher than ever, but since taking a stand on **civil rights** he had become a figure of hate across much of **the South**. Visiting Texas was part of an attempt to recover all the possible votes he had lost. He knew it might be unpleasant, even dangerous.

◀ *Lee Harvey Oswald, who almost certainly shot Kennedy. He was himself shot in police custody by Jack Ruby.*

Five hours later Kennedy was dead, gunned down by rifle shots while riding through Dallas in an open car. Lyndon Johnson was sworn in as president later that day, a dazed Jackie Kennedy standing beside him in her bloodstained clothes. She had refused to change them. 'Let them see what they have done,' she said.

Within hours, 24-year-old Lee Harvey Oswald had been arrested for the crime. Two days later, millions watching on live TV saw him shot dead by another man, Jack Ruby, as the police were moving him. Since that day there have been all sorts of theories as to who really killed Kennedy. **Organized crime**, the Cuban government and conspiracies of Southern **racists** have all been offered as possible suspects. The overwhelming weight of the evidence still supports the conclusion reached by the Warren Commission in 1964, that Lee Harvey Oswald, for reasons best known to himself, acted alone. Whether others were involved in a parallel plot remains an open question.

▲ President Kennedy's flag-draped coffin is carried past his veiled wife. She is flanked by Kennedy's brothers Edward and Robert.

51

▲ *Jacqueline Kennedy, John Junior and Caroline leave the White House for a service at the Capitol commemorating the dead president. Robert Kennedy follows them down the steps.*

John F. Kennedy was in the White House for less than three years, but these were some of the most eventful years in recent American history, and the young president faced challenge after challenge.

Abroad

Kennedy thought of himself as an expert on foreign affairs, but it was in this field that he experienced his greatest failures. Admirers have argued that the USA and the Soviet Union were on better terms when he died, and it is true that both powers had come to realize that they had no choice but to live with each other in peace. But the **arms race**, which he so wilfully accelerated in 1961, proved both destabilizing and costly for another 30 years, and his risking of human lives in the interests of American prestige during the Cuban Missile Crisis was almost inexcusable.

His policy towards Vietnam was muddled and ultimately mistaken. He might have cut short the American commitment had he lived – he certainly seemed, in the last months of his life, increasingly aware that such a war was unwinnable. But it is doubtful whether he fully understood why. Kennedy saw history as a story of great men making decisions; he never seems to have fully understood how the interweaving of political and economic processes creates situations. Vietnam, Cuba and the rest of the **developing world** were something of a mystery to him.

His one great success in this field was to undermine the old American tendency towards **isolationism**. Kennedy understood that everyone lived on the same planet. The world could not 'long endure the growing gulf between the rich and the poor', he said in 1963. An end to poverty was in everyone's interest.

At home

Kennedy's domestic record was also littered with failures, but here it was others' ignorance that was mostly to blame. Given the slender margin of his victory and the make-up of his own party, he always knew he had to tread carefully. 'There is no point in raising hell and then not being successful,' he said, and he followed his own advice. He just kept plugging away, introducing bill after bill, and arguing each case over and over again. During his lifetime, Congress rejected most of them, but ten years later programmes like **Medicare** would be taken for granted by most Americans. When it came to social issues, Kennedy was ahead of his time.

Kennedy was also cautious when it came to **civil rights**, but by upholding the law he and Bobby gave the movement the chance to push even more strongly for change. Once he realized that the momentum was both politically and morally irresistible, he put his own weight behind it, despite the inevitable electoral cost.

His famous civil rights speech in June 1963 marked the turning point. Like many of his speeches it was inspirational, and here perhaps was his true legacy. No matter how restricted his actual achievements, Kennedy's true legacy lay in what he said, and the mark his words left on the hearts and minds of his fellow Americans. In the end it was this legacy that made it possible for Lyndon Johnson to succeed where he had failed.

Last and first

When Kennedy died, World War II was less than a generation in the past. The Beatles were still unknown in America, and computers were still a novelty. In some ways he seems like the last president of an older age, one in which men made all the rules and war was still considered an acceptable way of solving disputes. He certainly did nothing to advance the cause of women, in either his public or his private life.

However, in other ways Kennedy can be seen as the first leader of the modern era. He was the first Catholic president of the USA, the first to fully realize the political potential of TV, the first to use 'spin doctors', or specialized spokespersons, to get his messages across. During his presidency another giant step was taken towards true racial equality in America, and this revolution in attitudes fuelled that wider outpouring of optimism and idealism that characterized the 1960s as a whole. If Kennedy did little to bring these changes about, he gave them a voice that was impossible to ignore.

▲ President John F. Kennedy at his desk in the Oval Office.

The promise

'The dream of conquering the vastness of space; of partnership across the Atlantic – and across the Pacific as well; of a Peace Corps for less developed lands; of education for our youth; of jobs for all who seek them; of care for our elderly; of an all-out attack on mental illness; above all, of equal rights for all Americans, whatever their race or colour – these and other American dreams have been vitalized by his drive and dedication. Now the ideals which he so nobly represented will be translated into effective action.'

(Lyndon Johnson, five days after Kennedy's death, promising to continue his work)

Timeline

1914	Oct	Marriage of Joseph Kennedy and Rose Fitzgerald.
1917	May	John Fitzgerald (Jack) Kennedy born.
1930		Enters Canterbury School, Connecticut.
1931		Enters Choate School.
1935		Begins course at London School of Economics.
		Returns to USA and enrols at Princeton University.
1936		Enters Harvard.
1937	Dec	Joseph Kennedy appointed US **Ambassador** to United Kingdom.
1938		Jack Kennedy does summer tour of Europe.
1939		Spends nine months in Europe.
1940	June	Graduates from Harvard.
	July	Publication of *While England Slept*.
		Jack Kennedy begins a year of study in California.
1941	Sep	Enlists in Navy, works for Naval Intelligence in Washington.
	Dec	USA drawn into World War II.
1942		Kennedy works as safety instructor in South Carolina.
1943	April	Arrives in Solomon Islands, takes command of *PT 109*.
	Aug	*PT 109* cut in half by Japanese destroyer.
1944	Aug	Death in action of Joe Kennedy Junior.
1945		Kennedy works as special correspondent.
1946	Nov	Elected to House of Representatives.
1947		Diagnosed with Addison's Disease.
1952		Meets Jacqueline Bouvier while campaigning for the Senate.
	Nov	Elected junior Senator for Massachusetts.
1953	Sep	Marries Jacqueline Bouvier.
1954		Undergoes two serious operations on his back.
1955		Writes *Profiles of Courage*.
1956	Aug	Loses vice-presidential **nomination** at Chicago Convention.
1957		*Profiles in Courage* awarded **Pulitzer Prize** for biography.
	Nov	Birth of daughter Caroline.
1958	Nov	Kennedy re-elected to **Senate** by record majority.
1960	April	Wins Wisconsin **primary**.

	May	Wins West Virginia primary.
	July	Receives Democratic nomination at Los Angeles Convention.
	Sep	Debates Richard Nixon on TV.
	Nov	Wins presidential election.
		Birth of son John.
1961	Jan	Kennedy inaugurated as 35th president of the United States.
	Mar	Formation of the Peace Corps.
	April	Landing of Cuban **exiles** in the Bay of Pigs.
	May	**Freedom Riders** begin their protest.
		Kennedy proposes to send a man to the moon by the end of the decade.
	June	Meets Khrushchev in Vienna Summit.
	Aug	The Berlin Wall goes up.
1962	April	Kennedy forces steel companies to abandon price rises.
	July	**Medicare** Bill defeated in **Congress.**
	Sep	James Meredith attempts to enrol at University of Mississippi.
	Oct	Cuban Missile Crisis.
1963	April	**Civil rights** (Freedom Riders) campaign in Birmingham, Alabama begins.
	May	Anti-Diem **Buddhist** demonstrations begin in Vietnam.
	June	Civil rights riots in Tuscaloosa, Alabama.
		Kennedy presents far-reaching Civil Rights Bill to Congress.
		US–Soviet 'Hot Line' agreement.
		Kennedy visits Berlin and Ireland.
	Aug	Birth and death of son Patrick.
		Civil rights march on Washington.
		Test Ban Treaty signed.
	Nov	South Vietnamese leader Diem overthrown and killed.
		Kennedy assassinated in Dallas, Texas.
		Lyndon Johnson sworn in as 36th president of the United States.
1964		Civil Rights Act passed by Congress.
1965		Voting Rights Act passed by Congress.
		Medicare Bill passed by Congress.
1968	June	Robert (Bobby) Kennedy assassinated in Los Angeles.
1969		NASA fulfils Kennedy's pledge to put men on the moon before 1970.

Key people of Kennedy's time

Castro, Fidel (born 1927). The leader of the **Communist** revolution in Cuba. In the Cuban Missile Crisis in 1962, Castro agreed to Russian nuclear missile bases being built on Cuba. These were removed after Kennedy blockaded Cuba and threatened Russian ships.

Eisenhower, Dwight (1890–69). American president from 1953 to 1961. Until 1951 he had been chief of staff of the US Army, but left to become the **Republican Party** candidate in 1952. Under his two-term leadership the Korean War came to an end.

Johnson, Lyndon B. (1908–73). Became vice-president to Kennedy when the latter was elected president in 1960. As vice-president, he automatically became president himself when Kennedy was assassinated in 1963. Johnson won the presidential elections in his own right the following year. He refused to stand for re-election when he lost popular support because he failed to end the Vietnam War.

Khrushchev, Nikita (1894–1971). Became first secretary of the Soviet Communist Party in 1953, and over the next few years gradually became the undisputed leader of the Soviet Union. He was supremely optimistic about the future of the Soviet system, but a combination of economic and diplomatic failures led to his peaceful removal from power in 1964.

King, Martin Luther, Junior (1929–68). One of the most famous **civil rights** leaders of all time. His 'I have a dream' speech in Washington, DC in August 1963 inspired millions of people across the world to campaign for civil rights.

Ngo Dinh Diem (1901–63). Became the first president of South Vietnam in October 1955. His oppressive regime, which featured his brother as chief of the political police, grew increasingly unpopular, and in 1963 he was overthrown and killed by the South Vietnamese military.

Nixon, Richard (1913–94). Vice-president when Eisenhower became president in 1953. Nixon himself stood in the presidential election of 1960, but lost to Kennedy. Nixon became president in 1968. He resigned in 1974 after a series of scandals.

The US system of government

Constitution
The USA is governed by its **Constitution**, a list of rules that were written down in 1787. Since then there have been 27 amendments (changes) to the Constitution.

Federal government
The **federal government** of the USA is based in Washington, DC. It deals with matters that affect all 50 states, such as national taxes, foreign relations, and welfare (social security). The federal government is made up of three branches: the president, **Congress** and the **Supreme Court**.

Executive – The president
The president is the head of the federal government and carries out the laws. He or she (though no woman has yet been nominated) is elected every four years. Since 1951 no president may serve more than two terms (eight years) in office.

Legislative – Congress
Congress is the law-making body (parliament) of the federal government and consists of two houses: the House of Representatives and the Senate.

Judicial – The Supreme Court
This is the highest court in the land, with nine judges, each appointed by the president with the advice and consent of the Senate. The Supreme Court has the power to decide if laws break the Constitution.

The House of Representatives – made up of 435 Congressmen/women, elected for two years

The Senate – made up of 100 senators (two per state), elected for six years

State government
Each individual state has its own executive (governor), legislative (senate) and judicial branches, based in the state's capital city. State governments deal with matters such as prisons, education, law and order, and local taxes.

Places of interest & further reading

Places of interest
John F. Kennedy Memorial, Runneymede Meadow, Egham, Surrey
TW20 9LS (an acre of land given by the people of the UK to the
USA in memory of John F. Kennedy)

John F. Kennedy National Historic Site, 83 Beals Street, Brookline,
Mass., USA (Kennedy's place of birth and childhood home)

John Fitzgerald Kennedy Library, Columbia Point, Boston, Mass. 02125,
USA

Websites
Educational website provided by the UK Public Records Office:
learningcurve.pro.gov.uk/heroesvillains/jfk

Heinemann Explore, an online resource for Key Stage 3 history:
www.heinemannexploresec.com

Website of the John Fitzgerald Kennedy Library and Museum, Boston,
Mass.:
www.cs.umb.edu/jfklibrary

Website of the White House (official residence of US presidents):
www.whitehouse.gov/WH/glimpse/presidents/html/jk35.html

Website of the US National Park Services:
www.nps.gov/jofi

Further reading
The Berlin Wall (New Perspectives series), Reg Grant, Hodder Wayland, 1998

The Cold War (20th Century Perspectives series), David Taylor,
Heinemann Library, 2001

The Cold War 1945 to 1989, Fiona Macdonald and Richard Staton,
Collins Educational, 1996

The Cold War, Josh Brooman, Longman, 1997

The Fall of the Berlin Wall (Turning Points series), Nigel Kelly,
Heinemann Library, 2000

The Vietnam War (20th Century Perspectives series), Douglas
Willoughby, Heinemann Library, 2001

Sources
John F. Kennedy, Lois Anderson, Bison, 1986

John F. Kennedy, Nigel Richardson, Evans, 1988

Kennedy, Elizabeth Campling, Batsford, 1980

Glossary

ambassador person in charge of representing their country's interests in another country

arms race competitive build-up of weapons by two or more nations

Attorney General chief legal official of the USA

balance of payments difference between what a country spends abroad and what it receives from abroad

blockade use of force to prevent goods reaching a particular destination

Buddhist follower of Buddhism, a religion of Asian origin

Cabinet in the USA, an advisory group appointed by the president, composed of government department heads

CIA US Central Intelligence Agency, which is engaged in gathering information through spying and other means

civil rights legal rights of all people to the same equal opportunities and benefits

Cold War uneasy peace which existed between the free enterprise and Communist worlds between the late 1940s and late 1980s

Communism the political and economic system of the Soviet Union, which featured centralized economic planning and government by a single party

Congress US law-making institution, comprising the Senate and the House of Representatives

conservative in the USA, someone who promotes private enterprise and responsibility rather than government support for the less well-off

convention party assembly at which the pesidential candidate is formally selected

counter-insurgency troops soldiers trained in fighting against guerrilla uprisings

deficit financing running an economy without insisting that income (money coming in) matches expenditure (money being spent)

Democratic Party one of the two major US political parties. During the Kennedy era it was considered to favour government intervention in economic and social matters.

desegregation ending of segregation (the enforced separation of races)

developing world the poorer parts of the world, principally in Africa, Asia and Latin America

economic embargo policy of not buying from or selling to a particular group or nation

exiles people living outside their own area or country

61

FBI (Federal Bureau of Investigation) department of the US government that investigates crimes to do with internal security

Freedom Riders organized group of civil rights protesters who set out to test the laws applying to racial desegregation on interstate public transport in the spring of 1961

free enterprise way of organizing the economy that relies on individuals rather than governments making the decisions about which goods and services are produced, and how they are bought and sold

Great Depression period of great economic hardship which began around 1929 and lasted for most of the 1930s

guerrilla fighters those who fight in a guerrilla war

guerrilla war war fought on one side by unofficial and irregular troops, often in difficult countryside

inaugural speech speech traditionally delivered by a new president after his or her formal acceptance of the office

inauguration formal acceptance of a new president to office

incumbent currently holding the position

isolationism policy of holding aloof from the affairs of other countries

liberal in the USA, someone favouring government intervention to aid the less well-off

Medicare in the USA, system of health insurance for citizens over 65 years of age

minimum wage lowest wage employers are allowed to pay

'missile gap' in the late 1950s, the (imaginary) Soviet lead in operational missiles

Nobel Prize annual international prize awarded for outstanding achievements in various areas, including peace, economics, literature

nomination choice made by a political party of one of its members to represent it in an upcoming election between the parties

political science study of politics

opinion polling organized investigation into how people intend to vote and why

organized crime groups of criminals who work together on illegal operations such as selling illegal drugs

primaries in the USA, local elections to decide who should receive local delegate support at the party conventions

propaganda release of information and ideas in such a way that only one side of a story gets told

proxy conflict dispute or war between groups who are also acting, deliberately or not, as representatives of wider groupings

Pulitzer Prize famous prize awarded each year in the USA for achievements in journalism and literature

racial discrimination treating people badly because they belong to a particular racial group

racism belief that individuals or groups are inferior because they belong to a different race to your own. People who do this are called racists.

Republican Party one of the two major US political parties. During the 20th century it was considered more sympathetic to business interests, and less inclined to support government intervention in social and economic matters.

rhetoric language designed to persuade or impress

running mate vice-presidential nominee

safe seat electoral district which a particular party (almost) always wins

segregation enforced separation of races

socialism set of political beliefs. There are many types of socialism, but all of them tend to concentrate more on the needs of the community and less on the short-term needs of the individual.

South, the in the USA, usually taken to mean those south-eastern states which made up the Confederate side in the American Civil War

state planning government planning of a national economy

stock market where stocks and shares are traded

strategic balance during the Cold War, the relative strengths of the Soviet and American nuclear forces

terrorists people who use violence and intimidation for political ends

unemployment benefits money paid to unemployed people by the government

voter registration drive campaign to ensure that everyone who can be registered is registered, and therefore able, to vote

Index

African-Americans 5, 43–7
Alliance for Progress 29, 31, 49
arms race 24–5, 52–3

Bay of Pigs invasion 30
Berlin and Berlin Wall 5, 25, 26, 27, 48, 49

Castro, Fidel 28, 30, 40, 58
CIA 28
civil rights 19, 21, 34, 43–7, 50, 54
Cold War 24, 27, 32, 48
Communism 19, 22, 24, 31, 50
Cuba 19, 30, 49
Cuban Missile Crisis 40–2, 48, 53

deficit financing 33
Democratic Party 15, 18, 19, 32
desegregation 33, 44, 45
developing world 22, 27, 28–9, 31, 49, 53

economic embargoes 30, 40, 49
education 32, 33
Eisenhower, Dwight 17, 58

free enterprise 24, 49
Freedom Riders 43–4

Great Depression 8

health care 32, 34
Hot Line (telephone link) 48

isolationism 53

Johnson, Lyndon Baines 33, 51, 54, 55, 58

Kennedy, Jacqueline (Jackie) 4, 16, 18, 36, 37, 51, 52
Kennedy, John F.
    anti-Communist views 24, 28, 29, 31
    authorship 10, 17
    death 4, 51
    early life and education 6, 7, 8, 9
    economic policies 19, 32–3
    education policies 33
    family background 6, 7, 11
    foreign policies 19, 28–31, 50, 52–3
    health care policies 34
    ill health 8, 9, 14, 15, 17, 38
    love life 12, 18, 38

marriage and children 16, 17, 20, 36, 37
    political science student 10, 11
    presidential campaign 18–20
    public speaking 18, 21, 23
    social policies 16, 19, 22, 32, 34, 53
    US senator 15, 16, 17
    wartime service 12–14
    working day 38
Kennedy, Joseph 6, 7, 10, 11, 15, 19, 34
Kennedy, Joseph (Joe) Junior 6, 7, 8, 11, 12, 14
Kennedy, Robert (Bobby) 7, 11, 19, 20, 21, 38, 42, 43, 44, 51, 52, 54
Kennedy, Rose 6, 7, 11
Khrushchev, Nikita 5, 25, 26, 27, 40, 42, 44, 48, 58
King, Martin Luther 19, 46, 58
Korean War 24

Laos 29

McNamara, Robert 20, 25
Medicare 34, 53
Meredith, James 45
Monroe, Marilyn 38

Ngo Dinh Diem 50, 58
Nixon, Richard 19, 58

Oswald, Lee Harvey 50, 51

Peace Corps 22, 23, 28, 55

racial discrimination 32, 43
Republican Party 19, 32
Roosevelt, Franklin Delano 11
Ruby, Jack 50, 51

Soviet Union 19, 24, 25, 26, 27, 29, 40, 41, 42, 48, 52
space race 27

Test Ban Treaty 48

US system of government 59

Vietnam 31, 50, 53

White House 36, 37
World War II 11, 12–14

Titles in the *Leading Lives* series include:

Hardback   0 431 13851 6

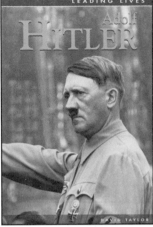

Hardback   0 431 13854 0

Hardback   0 431 13853 2

Hardback   0 431 13850 8

Hardback   0 431 13852 4

Hardback   0 431 13855 9

Find out about the other titles in this series on our website www.heinemann.co.uk/library